Hustler to Husband

By

Pastor Deshawn Jones

ALL RIGHTS RESERVED. No part of this publication may be reproduced, distributed, or transmitted in any form or by any means, including photocopying, recording, or other electronic or mechanical methods, without the prior written permission of the publisher, except in the case of brief quotations embodied in critical reviews and certain other noncommercial uses permitted by copyright law. For more information, please contact the publisher.

Copyright © 2019 Deshawn Jones
Published by Deshawn Jones

Acknowledgements

I would like to thank the Lord for the gift that he has given me (my wife.) You have always been my number one supporter in whatever I do. When my pen fell asleep, you encourage me to wake it up and go back to writing. From the time I seen you at the basketball game. I knew that you would be my wife. Thank you for believing in me, when I did `n t believe in myself. I love you Mrs. Jones.

Thanks to my two sisters (Vamesha Jones and Lakeisha West) for giving me approval to share our story. You guys are the best. This book is proof of the love that we had as kids, to now as adults. Thank you for your unselfishness with our story.

Thanks to my spiritual parents for grooming me into the man of GOD that I am today. Your lifestyle of integrity has taught me to be a better husband, servant, and leader. When I thought that church was n` t for me, you taught me that It was part of me (my purpose.) Thanks for all that you have done for my family. I love you Apostle Michelle and Elder Kelly.

Pastor Deshawn Jones

Dedications

In remembrance of my first love, the late great Rosa Jones my mother. This book is dedicated to you for birthing your only son. I count it as an honor to have spent 16 wonderful years with you. In your death, the pain taught me how to love again. I found hidden, strength, and learned how to forgive even when it hurts. As your son and your daughters, we are the legacy that you have left in the earth. To mirror what you looked like and lives that you impacted. R.i.p. mom, this book is for you.

I dedicate this book to some awesome guys that have encouraged and supported the vision that GOD has given me. You guys gave me that extra push when I got frustrated with writing. The phone calls, to the early morning texts helped me to stay focus. I dedicate this book to you guys (Antonio M. Byrd, Terrell Hawkins, Terrell Hurse, Vernon Reeves, and Quandrell F. Smith) we are not just friends, but you guys are my brothers. I have been pregnant with this book for years and through the love of many I have given birth to it. Thanks to the (Thahawkmedia) for this awesome book cover and my T. shirt line.

Thanks Rosie Delisca and Sandra Williams. You guys are the best. I dedicate this book to you both for helping me with the vision that GOD has given me to share with the world.

This book is dedicated to all who helped me develop to the man that I am today. GOD BLESS YOU ALL !!

Prologue

This book cover speaks to the transition of my life. From hustling, getting married, to preaching the word of GOD, going back to my hometown, and helping build back what I once destroyed as a young man. Where you start off in life it doesn't determine your outcome. This book teaches you how to continue in a course of action, even when you're faced with difficulty. It gives you hope in the place where you may have been drowned in doubt.

Your reward in life is in the pressing. The more you keep going forward, you will unwrap the gifts that life has for you. Most people run from pain and hardship. Life has taught me that the greatest battles are not won during the war. But you gain your greatest strength in the toughest moments. The way you prepare and execute gives you peace with the end result. We all go through process, but you must know that there is an expiration date to it all.

From Hustler to Husband

Sometimes in life we take the wrong turn by putting ourselves in situations that can cause hurt to our loved ones and ourselves. At that moment, we are not thinking about our family or future, we are just focusing on our own needs. For me it started when I was 16 years old. Little did I know my life was about to take a drastic turn. My mom discovered a lump in her breast. She didn't think much about it because she was young and full of energy. We were just an average family. My mom and stepdad were in the process of having a house built close to where we grew up at. As time went on, the lump in her breast begin to hurt. She went to the hospital and the doctors ran many tests to see what was going on with her.

One day, I came home from football practice and my stepdad said "Shawn, we need to talk." He explained to me that my mom had breast cancer, but he promised that everything was going to be just fine. We didn't know what breast cancer was at that time, but my family was about to find out firsthand. My mom began chemotherapy. I knew something was wrong. The things that she used to perform. Her strength was not there anymore to do them. It became noticeable when she cooked. A simple task of opening a jar of pickles became hard for her to do. Then her hair began to come out as she combed it. While cooking she constantly would sit down because she felt weak. Her weight began to drop rapidly and before you know it, she could not even get up from her bed. We ordered a hospital bed that gave her easy access to get in and out of the bed. My sisters and I were still clueless to the effect of this disease called breast cancer. Even though our mom was sick we still saw this beautiful, young, and loving mother who was holding on for the sake of her children.

    My cousin was a believer in JESUS CHRIST and she faithfully came over every day to pray and read to the bible with my mother. My mom was dying right before our very eyes. My sisters and I couldn't tell because we simply loved being around her and just thought she was very tired. When my mom first got diagnosed everyone kept telling us that she would be healed soon. So as children, we trusted their words. Being the oldest of the three, at times I could hear the pain in our mother's voice. A lot of the things that my mom did in the past, she wasn't able to do them no more. This frustrated her because the strength that she once had, was gone. Growing up, in my era, when an adult told a kid something, we took the weight of their word as true. Before the chemotherapy everything seemed o.k. with my mother's health. The treatment didn't prevent the cancer cells from diving and growing as it was design for.

    One morning my sisters and I were getting ready for school when my stepdad came into my room and said Shawn your mom just passed away. I knew my mom was getting worse, but I never thought death would be the end result. My heart fell to the bottom of my stomach and I began to cry. Then he walked out of my room and entered into my two sisters room. Moments later, I hear them begin to cry which hurt me the more. This made me angry and very upset with everyone. As a child I did not see this coming. I just remember everyone telling me that my mom will be better soon. I think, if they would have explained to me the truth about this disease in the beginning, the anger in my heart would not have been so bad. I understand that everyone thought that this was protecting me. But in the long run it left some inward hatred. The first person that I have loved. The person that always believed in me, was now gone. I understand we all have grandmothers and other family members who love us dearly, trust me it`s a different coming from the person that gave you birth. The connected from a mother to her child is priceless. *There is no love like the love of a mother.* This loss left me with so much pain on the inside. Feeling lost and confused, I took on an I don`t care attitude towards God and life. Later, I asked my family "why did you all lie to me?" I became this angry person at a young age and trusting no one. Several times, while sitting in my room I asked God, how could a person so young, die of cancer, being only 36 years old. I felt like throwing in the towel and giving up on life. I had a very close relationship with my mom. She believed in me so much. Especially, when it came to football. Everywhere we went, she would tell people that my baby is going to play professional football.

 Considering that I was the oldest of three, and being the only boy with two sisters, I felt that I had an obligation to fulfill. This was by far, the hardest thing I have ever faced in my young life at the time. I tried not to show hurt because I did not want my sisters to see me panic. When I was alone, the tears flowed like a fountain which lead me to asking God, why did you take my mother away numerous of time. She was young, a wife to be, loving, and always putting the needs of others ahead of herself. My mother was 36 years old, and now gone, leaving behind three children. I felt life was so unfair. My stepdad tried to take our mind off it with activities, but he could tell that we were all hurting on the inside.

Matthew 11:28 (KJV) says, come unto me all ye that labor and are heavy laden, and I will give you rest.

What we walked through, being so young gave us strength, comfort, and rest that we never thought that we had. That's why, as a grown man, not too much moves me. The loss of my mother matured me on how to handle tough situations. Which gave me an inner strength that spoke beyond my natural ability to overcome different trials and tribulations in life. To walk through something like this so young does something to you on the inside. As time passed on, the three of us got separated. We did not agree with the decision, but it was for the best. My mother was engaged to get married to my youngest sister's father and he was not able to take care of my two sisters. Being that they were young, and all the responsibilities that came with it, such as combing their hair, getting off early to cook, and giving them womanly advice. So, our grandmother raised who was my mother's mother my young sister and my other sister moved in with her dad to another city. I remain home with my stepdad so that he could raise me as a man. Life for the three of us was hard, but God had a plan. Here I was, young and heartbroken. It was not easy! The person you loved the most, the one that was your backbone all your life is no longer there to support you. My mom never got the chance to see me go to the prom, get married, or play football on a mature level. I had the support of others, but you and I know, it's not like the love of a mother.

As I write this book today, I stand stronger, wiser, and have more understanding. It is clear to me now that what we went through was part of our destiny. One person's pain is someone else's comfort, especially, when you have overcome what they are presently experiencing. As days turned into months, I felt like it was me against the world. My stepdad was working a lot of late nights and I had no one to talk with about what I was feeling. It really didn't hit me until I was at home by myself. Some nights I would sleep on the couch, only to awake to the voice of my mother. He never talked about my mom's death. I think he worked a lot, trying to take his mind off the reality of what happened. I dealt with the death of my mother by playing football and basketball.

The pain on the inside that I was carrying demonstrated outwardly by the way I punish my opponents in sports. Ecclesiastes 7:9 K.J.V tells us that anger rest in the bosom of fools. My mom's death shifted my entire life. Anger had my emotions out of control to the point that I couldn't manage my thoughts, which led to very bad headaches. I made a lot of foolish decisions during that time, because I was led by my head and not my heart.

TRYING TO FIND MYSELF

I started smoking marijuana with some of my childhood friends, thinking that it would ease the pain from the death of my mother. I was considered a late smoker. When my friends first started smoking I wasn't. My mindset was on playing professional football and I didn't want anything to get in my way or to slow me down from my dream. But when my mother died my dreams got altered. It was no longer a concern of me going pro. The very thing that I dreamed of as a kid went out of the window after the death of my mother. Smoking marijuana became a daily routine. I can recall My mom telling people "my baby is going pro". I was a very good football player. Playing football came natural to me. What took other guys long days of practice to accomplish, I could just walk on the football field and just do it. My talent was a gift from GOD. Football was my outlet to escape what I went through from the death of my mother. I would use the field to run away from my opponent as I looked at them as my problems. This was a way for me to block out what I was coming home to.

One day my best friend and I went to buy some marijuana. As I got out the car, I recognized one of the guys there. He was one of the helpers who used to help with our high school coaching staff. Immediately, I turned around to walk in the opposite direction. He called my name, "DeShawn" what are you looking for? I replied, nothing coach just riding through. He said, I know you came by here to buy some marijuana. I said, "no sir, I don't smoke." After going back and forth with him, I final said yes, I smoke. He said everything is cool. He then asked, how much money do you have? I replied, $40 dollars. He sold me a half of ounce of marijuana. I smoked it with my friends and as we were hanging out at an abandoned house, a guy walked by and asked who got the "smoke" that's what they use to call it. He said, sell me a bag. I did not know what to say. I grew up where I've witnessed older guys selling marijuana, but for me, selling it never came across my mind.

What happened next changed my entire outlook on life. I sold one sack of marijuana to the guy. And by selling it word got out that I was the weed man. I made $120 dollars from the marijuana that I purchased. This introduced me to a different way of living. It was like I became the weed man overnight. How could going to buy marijuana, turn me into being the "weed man". The next day, I called coach and said I don't know what happened, but I need more marijuana. He asked me again, how much money do you have? I told him $120 dollars. He gave me more marijuana and before I knew it, over the course of time, I was making anywhere from $500 - $1,000 dollars a day selling marijuana. I was trying to find myself through marijuana and ended up selling it. As time went on, I was purchasing 5 to 10 pounds a week. It is funny how the devil will detour you from your dreams and purpose only to get your attention, so you can do his business.

While all of this was going on, my stepdad had no clue of what I was doing while he was at work. He thought I was just playing football and going to school. When my friends' parents *were not at home, we used to bag up the marijuana at their house. Some of my friends use* to help me hide it when I got a big package in, for a small fee. The marijuana I had was the best around, plus my sacks was bigger than everyone else. I thought that I could not be touched. I was 16 years old with a pocket full of money, new clothes, and shoes daily. At times I had to hide the clothes that I bought at my grandmother's house so that my stepdad would not get suspicious. My grandmother thought that I was an angel and I would not do such a thing. Even when people told her that I was smoking marijuana, her reply was "my baby don't smoke!". Who would have thought that someone's life could change just in a few months' time? I was young, foolish, and blinded by the money from the marijuana. I could not see the plan of the devil using me to do his work. My coach and I developed a tight bond. I'm talking about him trusting me to the point of taking me to his house and showing me all his money plus the marijuana. If the police raided his house, what he had in there could have landed both of us **in** jail. We thought that we were untouchable. I was not aware that everything was about to take a downward fall.

One day, I came home from football practice. My uncle asked me did I hear what happened. I replied, no. He said, your coach got caught with a great amount of marijuana. I did not want to believe it, but I noticed that he was not at practice that day. Every time I called his phone, it went to his voice message. Later, I found out that it was the truth. A couple of hours later, he called me back. I did not answer the phone, I just let it ring so he would leave messages. Growing up in the hood we could tell when someone has got caught by the cops and was trying to cut their time by giving up the next person.

Through our relationship, I knew that I was one of his biggest buyers and the majority of the time in a situation like this the seller sets up the buyer to get less prison time. My phone kept ringing, so I finally answered it. We talked for a little while. I could tell that something was wrong from the tremble in his voice. I told him that I heard he got caught by the cops that afternoon. He replied, no man, I don't know what you are talking about. I told him, I'll call you a little later. He was persistent on meeting up with me so that I could make a purchase. My response was I will call you back. After I got off the phone, I threw my phone away. For the next weeks I chilled out and did not sell any marijuana. It was not hard for me to find a new connection because of the location that I was in. There were other guys that I could buy marijuana from. The life of a hustler continued. My new connect (the guy who I was buying marijuana from) price was even better than the price I got from my coach.

THE NEW WAVE

During the time that I lost my mother, I met this older guy who used to play basketball in my neighborhood who we called Black. Later we became good friends. He was very popular around the city. Over time our bond grew, which led me to calling him my uncle. He liked the way that I played hard nose basketball and football. I never backed down on the court or on the field. "Black" was like a big brother and father at the same time to me. The void place and relationship that I was looking for from my stepdad, he filled it. When I needed to go somewhere, he used to let me drive his car. I didn't know if he knew that I sold marijuana or not. So, at times I played the game as if I had no money so that he would give me some. Our friendship grew, the place where I had no one to talk with about the death of my mother now I had an ear to hear me. He wasn't that much older than me, but the streets have a way of maturing you fast. He knew I was a great athlete and he pushed me to be a better person. Because of that place I had a lot of respect for him.

As a man now, I understand the importance of a father speaking into the life of a boy. The words of a father shape the boy into the man he should become. It was beginning to look as I was getting back on track. My new connection from the marijuana was going well. From the new connection he seen that I was bringing in a lot of money and I was true to my word. Being young and playing ball had me feeling like a super star with the type of money that I was making. My friends and I was going to strip clubs, getting the V.I.P treatment, and hanging out with famous rappers. We were young, and I had the money to buy our way into any special event. A lot of the time older guys would just look at us like, who are you young guys, but when I pulled out the money, they allowed us to come in. That's when I got an understanding of the saying, "Money Talks." This was a big part of my teen years after my mother passed away. At a young age, my friends and I were experiencing what guys our age only saw in the movies. While guys our age was getting ready for school, majority of the time we were out hanging in the streets hustling.

Months later, I was riding my bike making a couple of stops in my neighborhood and guess who pulled up beside me? Yes, coach, he asked " where have you been" boy, I got some new stuff and it's the best in town. I said word on the street is that you got caught with a lot of marijuana. Of course, he denied it and said man this is your boy, you know me. He replied anyway give me a call, so we can get back in business. He gave me his number and as he pulled off, I said to myself "yeah right". I threw the phone number on the ground. Later that year, I noticed a lot of gang activities that was going on in my neighborhood. Two of my cousins had joined the gang and many of my friends from the other side of town were involved. There was one guy that stood out particularly to me in my neighborhood who we called O.G. A lot of guys respected him, and he was much older than the rest of us. He was out to recruit whoever in the hood that was looking to be down. As for myself, I was still doing my own thing hustling and trying to make my dream of playing professional football become a reality.

One day O.G. and I talked. Over time we developed a close relationship. Something that we both had in common was the hood. He loved the hood and I loved the hood too. One day he asked me to get down which means to (join the gang), but I told him that I'm good. I told him that I am a hustler, the gang life is not for me. A few days later I went to buy some marijuana from my new connect (drug dealer). I went to my aunt's house to bag it up. On my way to the spot where I hung out, the cops jumped out at me. I took off running until I was in the clear. One rule that we had was, if you are from the hood you should never get caught in the hood. You know in, the hood, (the police) just ride through. While escaping from the cops, I threw away my entire package. My plan was to sell everything quick so that I could re-up meaning (go get more) not thinking about the money but my freedom. Hours later, I went back to retrieve my package, but it was gone. I looked for hours but I found nothing. Now, I was frustrated! The money I spent was all that I had.

Well, O.G. from my neighborhood who was in the gang heard about what happened. He sent word that he wanted to talk with me. We met up, talked for a few hours. He respected the way that I carried myself. Little did I know this was part of his plan to get me affiliated. The book of Proverbs chapter 29 verse eighteen:

tells us, where there is no vision, the people perish. This place in my life had me perishing and the sad thing about it is I wasn't even aware of it. The enemy was blinding me with a lifestyle that was blocking the vision of playing professional football. This new wave was about to shift and shake the entire city.

TIMING IS EVERYTHING

I met with the O.G. from my neighborhood as I was about to leave, he gave me a large amount of money and replied you need to get back on your feet. I took the money, but I did not realize what just happen. This was the perfect timing to recruit me. He knew if he could land me in the gang, I would bring leadership, respect, power, and was trustworthy. Two weeks later I got down (join) in the gang and I was in full throttle. My mind set was that everyone already thinks that I`m in the gang, I might as well make it official. My street credit (respect) grew rapidly. I was a mastermind of getting away with crime and the influence on my life from sports had many guys joining the gang in our neighborhood. At the same time, my mentor (Black) had a federal case from selling drugs. I knew what he was doing, but out of respect I never mentioned it.

So, it seems as I had taken another loss, because I fed off the pain with anger and I was fighting a lot. As a little boy in my neighborhood boxing was a big thing that resulted into a lot of fights. Fighting for me, became normal. As a young boy, my uncle taught me how to fight. Before my mentor (Black) left to go to federal prison. He told me to be safe and he did not approve of what I was getting into. He knew that I would not stop, I was too deep in. In this new chapter of my life, if I could have seen in the future during that moment, I would have never taken the money from O.G. from my neighborhood. Boy, I tell you the devil really had me. The gang life brought violence everywhere we went. We had a core value that we were family. As a little boy growing up in my neighborhood, the older guys always taught us to have a tight bond. At that point of my life, the only thing that I loved was the streets and playing ball. I was so deep in the gang that I begin to put my street family before my own biological family. The streets had my mind so twisted. My uncles could see it, but I did not want to hear it when they mention it. There was even times that my uncles and I fought because of the decisions that I was making from the street life.

This new wave had me fighting more and more. It wasn't that I was fighting for my own self. A lot of guys always got into it with my cousins and living by the street code when one person in our group had a problem with you, we all did. Guys that I knew from sports became my enemies because their neighborhood and my neighborhood was at war.

John 10:10 (K.J.V) states… The thief come not, but for to steal, and to kill, and to destroy.

From this lifestyle, as I look back, the devil almost destroyed two generations with this gang life and is working on the third generation. The enemy knew that if he could kill us before we knew who we were; our families, sons, daughters, community, and city would have stayed divided. All of this took place in a matter of months after my mom's death.

One day, I decided that I was no longer going to stay with my stepdad. By him working all the time we did not see each other often. Losing a mother at any age can cause permanent hurt. Especially when you are just a child. That summer I can count on my fingers the number of times we saw each other face to face. Some nights I use to cry myself to sleep thinking about how we use to live there as a family. Now, it was just only me there to overcome a place that I wasn't t ready to face alone. I thought that I was grown because of the life I was secretly living. The enemy began to tell me, that he does not care about you. The older that I got, I realize how selfish I was. Never did I think about his feelings. He also lost a close friend and soon to be wife. He was just 34 years old at the time and now as a husband, I can imagine what he went through as a young man now, putting myself in his shoes with my wife of today. Sometimes we hold people to standards that we ourselves don't plan on living up to. I thought that this move for me was the best. As I look back it robbed me of so much more.

I moved with my grandmother but that did not last long. One of my uncles and I use to fight all the time. I wanted to hide what I was doing from my grandmother, so I moved in with my aunt. Now at the age of 17, I had so much going on while I was still playing football and was one of the best players on the team staring on both sides (offense & defense) of the ball. I receive the M.V.P. 2 yrs. in a row averaging almost 10 yards a carry and 11 solo tackles a game.

Proverbs 16:8 (K.J.V) Pride goes before destruction, and a haughty spirit before a fall.

Pride really had my head swollen. I was highly recruited by colleges such as The Florida Gators, South Carolina, Georgia Tech, Auburn, and many more Division 1 prospects which all have great football programs. They did not know that this raw talent came from the death of my mother, being involve in a gang, the street life, and a hustler. Football was my therapy to punish my opponents on and off the football field. Knowing that I was so close to going to the next level of playing football. In one day, I destroyed my entire possibilities of being a professional football player. This hurt so bad, B/C as a kid this was my dream. It was cut short from a bad discussion that I made. I ended my career before I could start my career. Timing Is everything, because for me I was in the wrong place at the wrong time. (1 Corinthians 15:33 N.I.V) Tell us, do not be misled, bad company corrupts good character.

I once heard someone say show me your phone and I can tell you where you would be in few years. A lot of times when we think that we have it all together. We tend to disregard intentionally the advice that is going to help us. An old man told me when I was out in the streets (hustling) "an old fool, use to be a young fool". That saying stuck with me from that day on.

YOU CAN BE YOUR WORST ENEMY

A few days later, I was charged with aggravated assault. This occurred because my uncle was fighting another guy and when I tried to break it up, the guy hit me. So, I begin to fight back. When my friends saw what was going on, they also engaged in the fight, hitting the guy with chairs and other objects. Afterwards I went home, and I did not think much about what had occurred. The next day, I attended school. While I was in my fourth period class, the assistance principle called my name on the intercom about 10 times in less than 3 minutes to come to the office. I gave my money to one of my friends and said man they are about to lock me up. Honestly, I thought it was a drug bust. As I headed to the office, a police officer was waiting on me. The crazy thing is that I had just passed the same arresting officer as I made my way to class. He asked me was I Deshawn, I replied "what`s going on" and he immediately put the handcuffs on my wrist. That was one of the most embarrassing moments of my young life at that time. Being popular around the school, I always walked with my head high and chest out. But at that moment after getting arrested, I was just a scared kid who wanted his mother. The bell to class had just rung and everyone saw me being put into the police car. I could hear the soft whisper of everyone asking, "what did he do"? I just held my head down in shame.

A witness told the cops that I acted alone. The incident resulted to me being put into jail for the hurt that we caused the guy who we fought. Anytime that you go to the hospital for an injury, caused by someone else. The state takes a warrant out on the individual who commit the crime. I was released the same night, and in that same week I return to the same jail for another aggravated assault charge.

What a look for an All-Star player. During that period, our High school football team was going through a transitional stage with the coaching staff. I believe the new coach wanted to make a name for himself. In the mist of all of that, I was going into my senior year. I was recently named an All American, but I got kicked off the team due to my actions. The pain that I had when my mother died return to me again. From not being able to play football killed me within. This was my outlet and now not playing crushed me. I lost my first love which was my mother and now, I had to deal with the idea that I can`t play football. Football was more than a game to me, it was the place where I could escape from the streets, the gang life, and the drugs. Being on the football field Is the only place that I felt safe. This was the only thing that kept me going. I had become my worst enemy. My own actions had resulted in me being kicked off the football team. I had become my worst enemy and I did not know it. This was a dangerous recipe for disaster.

The street life of hustling and gang banging was beginning to catch up with me from the bad seeds (action) that I had sown (done).

Galatians 6:79 (KJV) Be not deceived, God is not mocked, for whatsoever a man sow, that shall he also reap.

When you are doing wrong you never think about it making a full circle and coming face- to - face with you one day. Growing up in the hood, sports was the one thing we had to escape from the reality of where and how we lived. I wasn't only a good football player but I also was very good in basketball. My quickness, strength, and defense landed me with a starting role even on the basketball team. Two of my closest friends from the neighborhood also was starters on the team who was very good in basketball. They could shoot the ball from any area on the floor, they were "the truth" (very good). I played high school basketball for 3 years but the coach and I couldn't see eye to eye. For one thing he had a thing against football players and being a lover of football, I decided to make it my main priority. When I wasn't playing ball, it seemed as trouble would just to find me.

One time after a basketball game, a rival gang from the other side of town and my neighborhood got into a huge altercation that lead into a big fight. One of our guys pulled out a gun and started shooting, everyone quickly ran to their cars and drove off. If I only knew what was to come of this gang life. A couple of days later some of the same guys drove through our neighborhood and shot at a couple of guys. This escalated into a streak of shootings in our neighborhood to their neighborhood. This made the neighborhood so hot that the police use to patrol our area every other hour making it difficult for me to sell marijuana.

I had to come up with a different strategy of making money. So, I started selling crack and cocaine. What I made from the marijuana sell was nothing compared to the new drugs I was selling which tripled my money. The thing that I loved the most about selling crack and cocaine it was much easier for me to hide it, compare to the marijuana which had a strong smell. Remember the guy I met on the basketball court (Black) he turned out to be the big man with the drugs. I knew that he sold drugs, but I did n`t think he was doing it on that level. When he heard that I was selling drugs, he was like… man you going to do it anyway. I started to make my purchase from him. By this time, he was just getting out of jail and everything begin to change for me. He showed me the in's and out of cocaine. I began to develop a new fan base. With the short time of just playing ball to selling marijuana, to being in a gang, to now a drug dealer. If anyone would have told me three years earlier that I would be living this lifestyle, I would have said that you were crazy.

Life has a way of turning 360 degrees when you are faced with heartbreak. Not being able to play football had me smoking marijuana like there was no tomorrow. Every day I smoked marijuana to keep a cloudy (apathetic) mind so that I could live in the fog of what I was going through to hide my pain. I was my worst enemy causing hurt to myself, but no one ever told me. As I got older, I understood why. When people are benefiting from what you're doing. They will never tell you of your wrongdoing until it is too late. Most guys find themselves in jail or seeing the death of a love one before they notice what they were doing was wrong, now they have time to think. It's one thing to have an enemy and you are aware of it, but to have your worst enemy to live on the inside of you is another thing. My worst enemy was me and it caused a lot of pain to the people I loved the most (Family).

ALL ALONE

Some days I use to go to the cement pond to be by myself. This was a place where old concrete trucks were kept after they were wrecked. I used to sit there and think of my mom, sisters, and stepdad. I left home at 16 years old because I felt as if I was the only one living there. This why it is important for men to speak into the ears of their children. If you are not speaking in their ears, I guarantee that someone else will. What children hears, shapes their future and destiny. Have you ever seen a mother that had a son by a man who she used to be in love with? but as time passes, they became enemies. The son reminds the mother so much of his father that she begins to call him what the father did not accomplish in their relationship. If he was not a good provider, she would begin to speak down on him. By calling her own son lazy like his father or saying you will never be nothing just like your dad. Then before you know it, her words have shaped her son into what has been spoken from her mouth. When we are aware of the words that we speak and that It has life. We would be more careful of how we choose our words by naming people.

Proverbs 18:21(KJV) Death and life are in the power of the tongue, they that love it shall eat the fruit there of.

"Your tongue will prepare you for what you will eat in the future."

Immaturity will rob you of time when words are spoken out of your emotions. That summer I could count on my hands the number of times that I saw my stepdad. I was very active in football and basketball. Some days I would practice up to 5 times a day. I would wake up and go to football practice, leave there go to basketball practice, go home, and eat. Then repeat the same cycle without seeing my stepdad. The only reason I knew that he came home because whenever the food was low, he would buy more. So, one day I heard a voice tell me to leave. People used to tell me that he asked them was I a drug dealer or in a gang.

Feeling all alone had me investing more time into my new family, which was the gang and we became more ruthless in the streets. Wherever we went people respected us because they heard of the things that we were doing. What made us so dangerous was the love that we had for one another which led to loyalty and respect. Our entire clique consisted of young men between the ages of 13 -17 years of age. We were young with militant mindsets. Believe it or not majority of what we learned came from old school gangster movies that I used to watch. Most of our guys came from broken homes where there were no fathers, just single mothers. That's why today I believe in building up the man. I believe if you build the man, he will build the family, and the family will build the community, that will build the city.

When a father is not present in his son's life to tell him who he is, it leaves that son to look for someone who will tell him who he is elsewhere. A father introduces to a son who he will become. I was the oldest of the guys in our circle which made me a big brother and a father to many of the guys. The leadership that I carried on the football field just flowed over into the street life that I was living. People would always look to me for the answer and I noticed that it came natural to me. This lifestyle had me becoming my worst enemy.

A few years later the older guy O.G. from our neighborhood, *the one that introduced me to the gang life,* got arrested and had to serve some time in prison. His brother took his place and he was the totally opposite of him. O.G was more of talking situations out, but his brother shot first then asked questions later. He made more enemies and had the hood at war with many of other neighborhoods. So, we found ourselves beefing more than ever.

"IF YOU BUILD THE MAN, HE WILL BUILD THE FAMILY, AND THE FAMILY WILL BUILD THE COMMUNITY, THAT WILL BUILD THE CITY."

One day he got into an altercation with another guy that was affiliated with our neighborhood and it turned bad. He shot the guy which lead to bad blood between our neighborhood and theirs. Months later he got arrested and left us in a messy situation. It was crazy because the guy who he shot was close to us. With him also being locked up, the beef (fighting) escalated on a level that you could not even imagine. The dangerous part of it all, is that we live two blocks away from each other with a highway dividing us. Not to mention we both knew each other neighborhood like the back of our hand. We all came from the same set (gang) but when that incident occurred It caused a quick separation. Now the guys in the neighborhood looked for me to call all the shoots (make decision). They knew that I was a leader, I had respect, and was about the hood.

At the age of 18, I became the head guy in charge of my neighborhood with my right-hand man being my cousin who I knew always had my back and I had his. From that day forth, we did a lot and saw a lot from living the street life. The street life will mature you very fast whether you are ready or not. We were stuck in the middle of a war between guys that we used to be very close with. Making enemies makes it hard when you're trying to hustle. This cost me not only friendships but a lot of money. You begin to speculate who did this or that. It made you cautious, especially when there was a shooting or other gang activities that went on in the hood because of all the people we were at war with. Simply for the fact that we were at war with multiple different gangs. It got so bad with us living just two blocks away, every other night there was a shooting. We were always in a battle because majority of the time we went to the same places. We were once so close and now we are waring with one another. We could not be in the same location without something taking place. I felt bad for many of the guys that was with us. Being in charge, I had to show them that we were not going to back down from no one. Even with some of our older leaders in jail. These types of activities turned our small city into a war zone like major cities as Chicago, New Orleans, California, or New York. This beef went on a few years and it was very intense.

A couple of years later O.G. from our hood got out and we were thinking… now we will end the war at once. He was the type of guy that had influence on a greater scale than I had involving the gang life. We talked one day and from the conversation I could tell that he was on another level, he had a different plan. O.G. was not the same guy I met before he went to prison. The guys in the hood and I took it as a slap in the face. He did not want the beef no more, that his brother started by shooting one of the guys from the neighborhood who we were beefing with. The same guys that was trying to kill us, he now wanted to talk it out with them. Word got back to me that he met up with them privately and he acted like nothing happened.

His brother's actions cost my friendship with guys that I played ball with. It seems as he had forgotten about the hood the very thing that me and him had in common. I know as you're reading this book, you would say that he did the right thing. When you are so deep into this lifestyle it's hard to shake it. Even when you try to live a different life people will always remember what you have done to them or their family. The devil had us thinking death was the only way out. That's why we could n't accept the fact of him not joining in with what was going on. As time went on the shooting and fighting slowed down. At this point we distanced ourselves from him and did our own thing. Our neighborhood was very big so most of the time we stayed down at the bottom and O.G. stayed up at the top.

During that time, the Police department Gang Task Force passed a new law in our city calling it the Gang Law Act. They were looking for pictures of tattoos with gang signs to see who they thought were gang members. They were looking to make an example out of someone. We chilled out from all the waring and started to focus back on other things, but in the back of our minds we knew that life would never be the same between all of us. B/C of all the gang activities my name became known around my city. Once the police pulled me over. The person who they thought that I was, surprised them. One of the cops thought that I had someone else licenses. What they heard of me did n` t match my face. I looked like a little innocent teenager who just went to school and home. People knew my name, but they did not know me. A lot of guys had respect for us because they heard about all the things that we have done in the streets, seeing it firsthand, or by word of mouth.

THE ABSENCE OF A FATHER

When I left home at the age of 16, I did not just leave home. I left the covering that was there to protect me. When it rains, we use an umbrella to keep us dry from the rain. With everything I went through, you could say, I got wet because I was not under the covering of my stepfather. As a man, now I know that there were some things that my stepdad could have told me that would have saved me from a lot of situations that I put myself into. However, when you think that you are grown, and no one can tell you anything. Your bad decisions will cost you eventually.

Statistics shows that with the absence of a father it affects a child's development. From growing up in the streets, I have experienced this firsthand. With our young ladies, pregnancy occurs in their teenage years more frequently. Many young ladies, because of the absence of a father, look for validations through relationships with older men who reminds them of their father or their brother. So many of our young ladies are going through life trying to fill that voided place with sex, drugs, and even to the point where they are allowing men to abuse them. They have never experienced the love of a father. They take the abuse because of the fear of being alone. This Is one lie the streets teaches our young ladies.

1 Corinthians 13:4 (AMPC) Love endures long and is patient and kind, love never is envious nor boils over with jealousy, is not boastful or vainglorious, does not display itself haughtily.

That's why it's very important that the presence of a father exists in the lives of our young girls. As they mature to womanhood, the little girl will always hold the grown woman hostage from walking in her fullness as a woman. Fathers bring confidence and help establish a sense of security in daughters. The father validates and affirms the girl into womanhood.

For our young boys they look to sex as an escape, to fill the empty place of not having affirmations from their fathers. They figure sex validates them as a man. I can recall as a young boy the older men would tell us that we were not men until we had sex. So, we grew up chasing sex and only to find out that when we are mad as men, we still need a toy to come us down. As I even think back, being one of the older guys in the gang, I had to father many of them from a place where I needed to be fathered.

During the mid-1990's and early 2000's dating to when I was out in the streets. The U.S. Department of Justice report that children from fatherless homes account for.

- 63% OF YOUTH SUICIDES.
- 90 % OF ALL HOMELESS AND RUNAWAY YOUTHS.
- 85% OF ALL CHILDREN THAT EXHIBIT BEHAVIORAL DISORDERS.
- 71% OF ALL HIGH SCHOOL DROPOUTS.

- 70% OF JUVENILES IN STATE OPERATED INSTITUTIONS.
- 75% OF ADOLESCENT PATIENTS IN SUBSTANCE ABUSE CENTERS.
- 75% OF RAPISTS MOTIVATED BY DISPLACED ANGER.

These numbers are very high and continue to grow each year. It may be because we live in a society that promotes the absence of a father. Even to the point that in the urban neighborhoods the mother can only get assistance from the government if the man is not present in the home. This is a trick of the enemy to remove the voice of the man until his voice will have no more influence and authority in the home. So that the men becomes strange to the urban community household in the lives of his sons and daughters.

From Hustler to Husband the title of this book, I have witnessed what the streets can do to a boy without a father or male mentor. A few years ago, I saw my father for the very first time through social media. We were able to talk, and he answered some of the questions that I carried with me for 30 plus years. With my mom dying at an early age, I never thought to ask about him. Because my stepdad was the man who I looked up to as a father. It hit me after my mom passed away that I never knew my biological father. I felt like we needed to make up for lost time. Being a man now I had questions, that only he could answer. At this stage in my life, there was nothing that I wanted from him. We planned to meet up, but It did not happen. I found myself in a dark place and I was upset about a relationship that did not develop between us. I felt a place of abandonment all over again, taking me back to when my mother died and the emptiness of never meeting my biological father. I did not understand where this place of pain was coming from. Later, I learned that even when you may think that God has forgotten about you. He will always send a replacement.

Psalm 27:10 (KJV) states when my father and mother forsake me, then the LORD will take me up.

He has done just that, by placing a man of God In my life, my spiritual father. He Is a person who I can share my heart with and he in return shows me the true love of a father. When I first came to the church that I'm a part of today, during their welcome session for the visitors, he embraced me with a manly hug that I have never felt as a son from a father. He`s a man of few words publicly, but when he speaks, wisdom flows. He and my spiritual mom have helped me become the man that I am today. As I encourage and build up men from city to city, it's just the manifestation of what they spoke over my life. My spiritual mom spoke that I will lead men and help father them. It amazes me sometimes how the Lord works. Growing up I did not have a father when I needed one the most. Now the Lord is using me to father other guys who were in a similar situation or worse.

So many husbands, brothers, sons, uncles, and nephews have never experienced the love of a father due to their absence. Majority of them go into marriage and are still confine to the boy who never got introduced to the man he should become from the affirmation of his father. From time to time, the boy comes out of the cave and the wife becomes puzzled to see a behavior that she never witnessed before in their marriage. The wife thinks that his age and size determine his maturity, but his actions are from what he did not receive as a boy in training to become a man from his father. Most guys imitate the male guy they are around the most, respect and trust. A father's voice shapes who that son will become.

    Growing up without a father causes most of my friends and I to look up to the neighborhood drug dealers to shape us. We saw the money, respect, and cars and thought that this is what makes a man. Very rarely you would see men in our neighborhood work an honest 9 to 5 job. With many of them going to jail, it made it no easier. When they get out of jail, the guys would have parties for them, give them money, and the ladies would be all over them. As young men we thought this was a win, win situation. If you go to jail and get out, you would be celebrated as a star. This why we need fathers in the lives of young men to teach them the truth about manhood. I have some friends that had a father in their life, and they were running from them. Guys like me did not have a father was running to what they ran from. If there's no father in the homes, you will understand the importance of having one when he's present. If we had more men telling our youth what to do. Many young guys would have never entered into a system that they are still facing years later.

    Fathers, I want to encourage you to step up and be who God called you to be to the family. My stepfather told my younger sister after his mother died, that he understood what we went through 22 years ago when our mother died. It hurt me to hear them words from him. For years, the feeling that my two sisters and I have been holding in our hearts was passed over to him. When his mom died our pain became a reality to him of what we have been feeling. His mom was a lady who I loved dearly and called my grandmother. The day that my mom died she and my grandmother were the first people there to comfort us. As a man who is grown with his own family. The Lord began to show me that every man needs another man when he's going through life situations. A real man understands the silence of another man. It costs a lot to be a man when you grew up without a father.

IT`S MORE IN YOU THAN YOU THINK

One day I was just walking in my neighborhood smoking weed and I ran into my best friend mom. I tried my best to hide the marijuana, but the smell was evidence that I was smoking. She said Shawn, you know if your mom was alive, she would not approve of what you`re doing out here in the streets. It was n`t that she seen me, but what she heard. I just had level of respect for my elders. Even though I was living wild, I still respected them. Then she said I know your mom raise you better than this. As she left, I kept walking while smoking, the words she said hit me in the heart. I have never had no one to remind me of how my mother raised me. This made me think long and hard to myself, because I knew there was more in me than this. While growing up, we probably were some of the only kids taking family vacations from our neighborhood. Where other kids just went to the local camp for summer. Our family was vacating. The pain of my yesterday turned into years of me losing myself in the streets, gang, and hustling, before I could see into my future. I began to cry out to God saying I got to get my life back on track.

During that time, I did not know God, but just knew of God. That conversation with my friend's mom echoed through my head from that day forth even while I continued to hustle on the block. It was more in me than I thought. Not dealing with my hurt started to affect the people who hung around me as well as myself. I grew up where the men in my family did not hug or show affection as men. As a teenager, it robbed me of my emotions. If I had known then that our tears are to refresh the inward man so that we can breathe again, I would had cried even more during this time. Crying Is a therapy that helps the intellectual process of the mind.

All along, I was making excuses for my dysfunction, that had me dysfunctional. As people, we tend to blame others when we are faced with adversity and look for fault in everyone else instead of taking responsibility for our own actions. Before all of this took place, I still was playing football. At the same time my High School head coach was taking a new coaching position in a different city because the principle and him did not get alone. That same year we went to the play offs and lost by one point to a team that was seeded at 1(the top team in our division) and we were the 6th seed (one of the last team to make it in). This was an easy way for our principle to use our loss as an excuse to fire our coach for lack of production. I had a real good relationship with my coach to the point that he wanted me to come alone with him. Coming from my background and seeing how he was raising his kids I did wanted no part of it. Once he made his son sleep on the back of his pickup truck while he brought his grade up from a 93 to a 98. My coach knew that I had the skill set to play on the next level (pro) and he did not want to see me end up as a statistic.

Good as it sounded, I could not move with him. My immaturity had me thinking that I needed to stay home and to lead the people that understood me. Going from an ALL AMERICAN in football, a hustle, and gang banger. I did a lot that I'm not proud of. I begin to look beyond my present stage. First it started with me going back to school. I dropped out of high school several times in my senior year and so I had something to prove again to myself. The events of life come at you so quick, but no matter what happens you got to KEEP PRESSING.

Even though I was doing all of this when I was in High School, I never made a failing grade. I earn my High School diploma with all the odds were against me. Walking across that stage proved to me that there was more in me than I thought. You never know what's on the inside of you until you have nothing else to stand on. I used to say to myself, what example I am being for my two younger sisters by not going to school? At this point of my life, I still did not know what God had planned for me, but I knew it had to be more than this lifestyle of living the street life.

Growing up in the projects I have observed guys that was gifted in sports, in academics, but remained within the project walls. I would always talk with the guys from my neighborhood who was some of the best athletes in our city. Telling them that your best players are not in the professional league. They are the guys that you pass by daily, but not aware of the talent that they possess. I have played and witnessed guys with talent such as Barry Sanders, Bo Jackson, Michael Vick, and a host of other great players. With none of them making it to playing professional ball.

Even when my life was n`t in order. I used to ask drug users how did they end up on drugs? In my neighborhood we had some guys that was so good in basketball that they could have played pro, but they ended up being victims to drugs. Growing up in the projects seeing drug users was common. It taught me to have a strong mind so that I would not be a victim of the product that I was selling.

One of the things that all of us had in common was sports. It did not matter what their addiction was, when it came to playing basketball on the court you could see the skill set and fight to win in each person. Our neighborhood was known as one of the toughest places to play ball, because of the talent level. At one point our basketball court use to be so packed that over hundreds of people use to come to watch us play. If you lose one time, it was a possibility that you would not play no more that day.

At the age of 20 years old The Lord began to work on me. While attending a High school basketball game I saw the most beautiful woman ever. I whisper to myself I got to have her. She was a gift sent from heaven to me. She was humble, caring, loving, understanding, and did I say BEAUTIFUL. This young lady reminded me so much of my mother with her personality. At the time I did not know it, but one of the methods God uses to save men from their own self destruction, is by sending him a woman. Even when he said that it was not good for man to be alone. As kids we were next door neighbors. She stayed directly in front of me. I got her number from one of her friends and the rest was history.

The more time we spent together the less time I hung out with my friends. A lot of them did not like it, because I was not in the hood like I use to be. Everyone noticed the change in me that was taking place slowly. I still was active in the gang and drug dealing but it was not my only focus. In (Genesis 24:67) it talks about after the death of Isaac mother Sarah, that he took Rebekah and she became his wife and he loved her and was comforted after his mother's death. I can relate firsthand because with my girlfriend at the time and later becoming my wife, I felt the comfort of LOVE. This young lady had my attention and I experience a love that I have never sensed before. She could care less about who I was in the streets or the drug money. She loved me for who I was which was very rare, majority of the time people hung out with me because they knew I would buy whatever they wanted or came around just for their own personal needs. When I gave her money to buy something nice for herself, she would buy me things. I said to myself this lady really does love me. By the time that people knew that we were dating, two years had already passed. People talked against our relationship to her because of my lifestyle, but we had a bond that was unbreakable. When I was with her, I felt a safe place. I could share my heart with her and for a guy to open his heart, safety has to be established. A man will never show his treasure to someone who he does n`t trust. She knew the things that I did and the lifestyle that I was living. One thing that made me love her the more was that she never, never judged me. I was happy for the first time since the death of my mother.

The bible tells us… "As a child I spoke as a child, I understood as a child, as a child, I thought as a child, but when I became a man. I put away childish things." It was more in me than I thought. I knew of The Lord, but I did not yet know The Lord. I could feel him shifting my life. My thought process was beginning to change, even my appetite from the things I use to do. Every day we spent more time together, developing a strong bond with each other. Three years later my girlfriend at the time was looking for more in life and did not want to be stuck in a cycle that leads to a dead end, so we moved to Florida.

THE TRANSITION

My girlfriend wanted a fresh start to escape from the old things that we were custom to. She knew that it was more to life than where and how we were living. I agreed with my heart, but in my mind, I was set on finding a connection with some big drugs. Growing up in Georgia one of the greatest perceptions we had was that Florida was the state for big drug connections. At first, moving to a different state was hard for me. I felt like a pilgrim in a foreign land. Majority of my family was in another state, but I knew that this was the best move for me. I did not tell anyone but my cousin and aunt at that time that I was going to move. My intention was to find a connection and meet my cousin at the Georgia / Florida line to give him the drugs. It`s amazing that we can have all our T`s crossed and I`s dotted and the plan does not go as planned.

Our mind set was focused on our purpose for moving to another state and to better our lives. My girlfriend got involved in the church, but I was not feeling it. She wanted me to experience the Lord on the level that she was on. I was not feeling it and church never crossed my mind. I started working with my girlfriend's cousin boyfriend, the money was n`t adding up. The manger told me I would make a certain amount of money, when I got my check it told a different story. At the time I use to ride with my girlfriend cousin boyfriend to work and one morning he did not come pick me up. I did n`t think much of it but he left me intentionally. The next day I went to work and notice that he was not there. He came to work about an hour later and said someone stole his car. His first response to me was, why didn't you come to pick me up? my responds was, I have not heard from you in 2 days. So, our friendship changed because of misunderstanding. Later I found out the reason he did not want me to work with him. It was because some illegal activities were going on.

    I came home from work that day and said I got to find a better job. One with better pay and benefits. I went online and began to fill out applications. No one called me for weeks and I began to get frustrated with the whole idea of moving out of state. So, I called my cousin to come pick me up from out of state. My plan was to go back, hustle, make a few thousands of dollars and come back home to Florida. During those weeks, I went to school and got my C.D.L licenses to drive trucks. Most of the companies wanted me to drive over the road, but I didn`t want to leave my family at night. I saw this ad in the paper for a local C.D.L. driver and I gave them a call. This took place on a Thursday and the company called me early that Friday. They wanted to know when I could start, and I replied Today! Later that Friday I went to take a drug test and did an interview which well. They wanted me to start that Monday. I forgot that same day my cousin was coming all the way from out of state to pick me up. I did not know how I was going to tell him the news of me not leaving and starting a new job. When my cousin got to my house, I told him about the job that I was going to take. Where I thought that he would be upset, instead he understood the reason why that I had to stay.

Sometimes the enemy tries to discourage us so that we won' t stay focus on what' s in front of us. If I would have left at that moment, I`m convince that this book would have never exist. The job that I have today is the same one I applied for over 16 years ago. It was a transition that was taking place right before my very eyes. Life was going great, my girlfriend and I got married. When you are living a life of hustling and gang banging you can never get a good night of sleep. The reason why is that you don`t know when the cops are going to kick in your door or if robbers are coming to rob you. A lot of what you see on T.V. when it comes to drug dealing. It happens in real life with guys going to jail or getting killed. What I escaped away from many don `t get a chance to tell their story, instead they become it through the eyes of others. This transition has taught me who I was alone the way. My wife and I both had a mind set to work and accomplish goals for our family. We were determined to build something new.

Then a few years later, the very thing that I moved away from presented itself before me again. Remember I had a plan to find a drug connection. Guest what? I found one. The guy was very low key. He was a helper on my job that assisted the drivers with materials that we had to off load from the work truck. One day we worked together he begin to share with me that he had a big boat that held about 20 people and he wanted me to take a trip with him to Cuba. It sounded good but I knew it had to be more to the story. Come to find out he was smuggling people from Cuba to Miami. It's amazing, when you are trying to do the right thing how the devil fights to keep you stuck in the familiar place. Even though this was my plan, when I got this job, my mind set changed. I was making good money and had awesome benefits. I told my wife and she was like Shawn are you crazy. She was everything that I was looking for in a woman and most of all I respected her too much to do anything without letting her know. I never took him up on his offer but remain focus on my transition. During your transition, the evil will always present itself. The enemy will lie to you, saying that the familiar place is where you belong. During this process I have learned moving forward is a mindset of the heart. (Proverbs 23:7 AMPC) tell us, for as he thinks in his heart, so is he. Your thought give birth to the impossible. If you can believe it, you can achieve it.

Days went on and my wife stared to get more into her bible. I woke up to her talking about the word of God on the phone to friends. I would come home from work and the only thing she had on her mind was JESUS. Her relationship with God was so intense that she was saying Shawn you need JESUS! The more she tried to push it on me, the more I put up a wall of resistance. The main reason I went to church at that time was to keep her quiet, so she would not ask me to come. I had a wall up from anything that had to do with the church. From the lifestyle that I came from and losing my mom to cancer at a young age made it hard for me to believe in God.

Death can hit you at a young age that will leave a mark on your heart that even time can't heal. Most guys my age that I hung with had not experience what I went through so young. Even though they saw the smile, but they could n`t see the hurt behind it. One thing I learned from it all is how to fight even when faced with adversity. Pain introduced me into who I was. My wife never stopped praying for me and that one day I would seek for a personal relationship with God. She realized that the more she was trying to push God on me, the more I distanced myself emotionally from her. Later, I learned that the Lord told her to stop trying to force him on me and just allow the love of God to demonstrate his glory. One of the worse things that you can do if one spouse is saved and the other one is not. You got to show the love of God instead of forcing it. Remember God is a gentleman he will never force his self onto no one. The Lord gave my wife divine instructions on what to do with me as I slept one night. He told her to blow into my mouth that night as I slept. In the natural mind I know you may be saying that this makes no sense. To be honest, I was the same way. When I woke up the next morning, I thought it was all a dream.

While driving my work truck it hit me that she was blowing in my mouth. I asked my wife that morning as we talked on the phone, did you blow in my mouth as I slept last night? She never really gave me an answer. I said to myself, this girl has gone crazy with this JESUS stuff. The things of God is foolish to the natural mind and especially when you're not operating in the spirit. At the time I did not understand it. Later, God reveal that it was a new wind of his glory that was about to hit my life. He used my wife to blow into my mouth as a sign of restoration and newness. God had a different plan for me all along. It had nothing to do with me being a gang banger, drug dealer or a professional football player. Everything that I went through developed me into who God called me to be.

    For the first time I understood why I did not go to prison, to even protecting me from the gun shoots when people were shooting at me. Numerous of time I have shot at people, shot people, and got shot at myself. Three times less than 10 feet away. It had nothing to do with me, but the purpose that God has for my life. It seen as my life would be another tragic story line, but God put it in a message for his glory to reach others that`s living that lifestyle. Many guys give up B/C they never see no one they know escape that way of living. So they embrace prison or whatever comes with it. That`s why God will use the overlook, to be looked upon for his name sake.

Matthew 22 :14 states for many are called, but few are chosen.

    All the while from my mother`s womb God had his divine hand of protection on my life. Some of the same things I did others got caught and served time in prison for. I was considered the worst one out of my all the guys in my neighborhood growing up. I could never understand why God kept me instead of the other`s. If I was drafted into the professional league, my mind set was all about the hustle, so you know what I would have done with the money. It is true that Gods ways are higher than our ways.

What happened in my life were just part of the process to help develop me for where God was about to take me. Process is defined as a series of actions. It started from the death of my mother, to selling marijuana, to joining a gang, and getting kicked off the football team which was part of my process. At times we get so caught up in the series of actions of life that we forget that all process has an end. This walk was teaching me that what we go through is just temporary and God sees us as the finish product. Transition and process work together to birth maturity. All along I was just an instrument that God was using to play sweet melodies to the ears of many to get their attention. What we go though in life is not for us. It is to help others so that they can overcome, because God used you to be a testimony to others that will face what you have overcame.

Trust me somebody is waiting on your testimony. All that I went through I still had a dream of playing professional football. I was working out to get my body in football shape, but every time I get ready to go and try out for a professional team something would happen to block from going. Later the Lord spoke to me and said son I did not call you to be glorified by this world, but by my kingdom. I shall use you to save many who have been through what you have gone through. Gods plan was for me to be a husband, father, a disciple for CHRIST, who would represent him for his glory. Back when I use to go to church with my wife, I was going only to keep her quiet, but now it was something different taking place in my life. I was n`t the same guy that I was when I first relocated from the city that I`m from. The Lord was changing me from the inside out and there was a (THE TRANSITION) taking place within me.

HUNGRY FOR THE LORD

There was a hunger that I had for God. Finally, I had an understanding that it was him all along that kept me, even in the mist of all that I been through in my life. My wife and I went to a few churches before we were able to call one our home base. It was a mega church. The way that they explain the word of God and broke it down was different from what I experienced back in my hometown as a youth. It started off good for me. As time went on, I really was not learning and growing like I thought that I should have. My spirit was looking for something that would refresh me even though I did῾ n t know what it was in the natural. We decided to go to another church. We founded one that was smaller but had a family atmosphere. The pastor and I related to each other in many ways, one of them was football. He was a chaplain for one of the local High school teams and he also helped with the coaching staff. He invited me to a football game which opened up a door for communicating between us. This was important B/C I was a person who always stayed to myself. Our relationship began to grow. I found myself hanging with him more and this man of God had great wisdom. To the point where, he was a recognize mentor for some members of the F.B.I. He used to meet with the men in his church every Saturday and he would pour into us.

    Another reason we connected so well was because he loved my B.B.Q. Every time I cooked on the grill he would stop by my house. We would eat and in return he released wisdom to me. I begin to help around the church because I was seeking for a deeper relationship with the Lord. Whenever we had service, I was right there. My sound was beginning to change, and my family back home could tell that it was something different going on with me through our conversation and my attitude. All this time I was trying to hide the pain that I felt from the loss of my mother, and not able to play football, to living the street life, was from a place of being empty. There was only one thing that could fill me up and that was JESUS himself. I tried all of what the streets could offer me, but still walked away broken and empty. This hunger I had from my experience with God opened the eyes of my understanding. There was such a fire on me that I would take notes on every gospel preaching. The more I ate from the teaching of the man of God, the more I wanted the Lord.

    Everything was going good until one day he preached on men having dread locks. It was another guy and I at the time in the ministry who was the only two in the church that had dreads. After that service, I noticed that the man never come back.

Proverbs 18:19 (KJV) tells us… A brother offended is harder to be won than a strong city.

I learned over the years that *Wise* men are not always wise. The message had no effect on me like it did the other guy. I had a hunger in me that kept my mind focused that nothing could get in the way of me learning about GOD. By now my dreads had gotten very long to the point when I went to sleep and tried to get up, it would pull me back down. When I went to get my dreads retwist it would take 2 hours. This was very annoying. So one day we were about to visit Georgia. I told my wife that I was going to get my hair cut. She couldn't believe it because my dreads were so long.

When we arrived in Georgia, I took my wife over to her aunt's house. I went to the barber shop. Walked in and told the guy that I wanted my dread locks cut off. He said, are you sure? Thirty minutes later I had a low cut and got up out the chair feeling like a new man. When I went back to pick up my wife, her mouth dropped. She was in shocked and surprised to see that I really did cut my hair off. This was something that I wanted to do for myself. When we went back home that Wednesday and attended church. The pastor said, now I can use you. Those words hurt me so bad. For a person of that level to allow someone hair style to determine who they are is shameful. As a man of God today, many guys tell me that this is one reason they don`t go to church. They feel as people judge them outwardly for what they have on, instead of getting to know the man inside of the clothes. I felt all along that he was judging me by appearance and not by my heart. It seemed as if he was more concerned about what others would think of me serving in his church with dreads. I truly did serve this man of God faithfully and with a pure heart. For him to say those words it cut me to the core. I was seeking for JESUS and met flesh. Slowly, I stopped going to church and I had the mentality that all church people were hypocritical. They say come as you are, but they judge you according to appearance. I came in wanting to learn about God but ran into ego and pride. For about a year I stayed out of church. The hunger that I had still was there. I just could not find the right place to feed me spiritually.

One day my wife and I was taking our daily walk around our neighborhood. A young couple approached us about a community outreach event that they were having. My wife stopped and talked with them, but I kept walking slowly. I was not ready to go back into any type of church setting. A couple days later my wife went to the event, but I drop her off and return home. When I came back to pick up my wife, one of the pastors tried to talk with me. I had a deaf ear from what I experience a year ago in church. My wife said that she was going to attend one of their Sunday service because she enjoyed the outreach event.

When my wife came home, she said that I would like the church and it was a friendly atmosphere. So, I went and the word that was preached in the house revived the hunger I had at the other church that we left. I start attending the prayer service, bible studies, and Sunday services. The people loved on a level that I have never seen or experience coming from church people and it scared me. I used to think, how could people love you so much and not know you. The pastor of the church talked with me one day after service. She asked why do I leave so early after church? I still had a wall up for protection, so that my heart would not get crushed again. Church hurt is one of the toughest things to bounce back from, but it can be done. I told her that I was going home to watch football. From that time forth I found myself staying later and later after service. One day I came on a Tuesday night and they were praying the walls down. I have never heard anyone pray on that level calling heaven down on earth. God was doing a new thing in us and it could not be explained. God had to redirect us back to a church. He knew what was in the church we needed it for what's to come in our walk with him.

A HEART OF STONE REPLACED WITH A HEART OF FLESH

As the praise team song before the Lord on a Sunday service, I begin to weep like a baby. Every bad thing that I had ever done in my past from the street life started rehearsing in my mind. The sound of worship challenged me to go back and visit that place so that I would not hold myself hostage and others that I have done wrong. The streets made my heart so cold and I never thought of the consequences when I committed these acts. My heart had become so hardened from losing my mom at a young age. That lead to a lifestyle of crime because of the hurt that had been covered up from years of inward emotions. I did not know what the Lord was doing. I could tell it was shifting my life and my wife could tell as well. She never had to ask me if I was going to church any more. She could see my actions, which spoke differently from the past. It was like a fire that shot up in my bones. I begin to care for people by demonstrating it with hugs and even crying.

This was new to me. Growing up, the men in my family never hugged or showed emotions. As a young boy, I was taught that real men don't cry or show affections. They said it was a sign of weakness. This lie has robbed a lot of men from expressing himself as a boy. Which we see in society today as men has replace feelings with video games. B/C as a boy they never showed emotions but learned how to act as everything is fine. This have caused many men to die in silence from emotions held inward that was never release as a boy. Something that is simple as a hug has deprive many men from expressing love to their sons. That's why many guys look for it in the streets, in drugs, sex, and anything that will fill that void place for the time being. One reason that I kept going to that church, was because one day the father of the house embraced me as a son. Every man looks for validation by a father to prove that he has arrived as a man. We see men in their 50's and 60's trying to replace their youthfulness with fast cars and younger women. The boy has been confined in the men and we see in many situations that the boy is screaming, let me out! As men we cover our feelings with things. We exchange our pain for joy of the moment. When no one is there that temporary joy turns into tears.

The streets teach our men to show no type of affection and it's killing our youth. This wall of hardness makes it difficult for so many men to cry and show love. The Lord is raising up fathers, uncles, brothers, and cousins who are not afraid to show emotions or cry in front of the kids. This teaches them the place of brokenness and dependency on GOD. I had a hunger and zeal for God that I could n' t explain. God had changed my appetite. I was seeking for him in the mid night hour, early in the day, and even listening to the word through my bible app daily at work. Day- by-day, I notice my heart was changing. I began to open the chambers of my heart, letting people in. For the first time, I felt as if this was a safe place for me to let people in. Guys that I used to shoot at and who used to shoot at me, we are now friends. Today, I talk with some of the guys on the phone and even pray with them. I realize God used that place for me to witness to the same guys that knew me as an enemy to now as friends.

    The years of living the street life can really alter your heart. You learn how to grow thick skin and to trust no one very quick. The LORD has giving me a heart of flesh now. With things that never used to concern me, now has become a burden on my heart to help people. I can feel the shift of caring for people to the point, that I pray with them. For they too can let go of the street life that I used to endorse. It was like a breath of fresh air. I could now inhale and exhale without worrying when I will go to jail or if someone was trying to take my life. It`s amazing when God blows on you. It will shift your entire direction and other people will notice it as well.

Proverbs 21:1(KJV)...*The king`s heart Is in the hand of The Lord, as the rivers of water. He turns it whithersoever he will.*

    When the Lord begins to turn your heart, it doesn't matter what you have been through, even if you think life dealt you a winless hand, God can change it suddenly

AM I REALLY SAVED?

The Lord tells us in his word according to 1 John 5:13: These things have I written unto you that believe on the name of the son of God; that you may know that you have eternal life, and that you may believe on the name of the son of God. Many times, I see people come to the altar, they give their life to Christ. In the past, I've heard people say that everything is going to be O.K. now that you are saved. Then two weeks later or less the same individual has gone back into the world and becomes worse than they were before coming into the house of The Lord.

I'm quick to tell people now when they become saved, "stay connected to well-seasoned people in the church." If it's a man I try to stay connected with him. If it's a woman, we point them into the counsel of our strong women in the church. A lot of times people get saved and doubt the very assurance of them being saved. Doubt is to your spirit; what pain is to your body. Pain gives us a warning signal when something is wrong or not balanced in our body. If the truth be told, a great number of people doubt from time to time. A double minded man is unstable in all his ways. Doubt comes to push us away from the reality of the true word that has been spoken. A way that helped me to block out doubt and focus on the Lord was intense prayer. Staying before the Lord, reading his word, and listening to my favorite preachers encouraged my spirit.

God did not send his only begotten son to disapprove us, but to save the entire world. Doubt is one of the tricks the enemy uses to play on our minds. He knows it is the mind that we serve Christ Jesus and if he can bring us out of our spiritual location, he can cause us to faint in our faith. When I first got saved, the enemy would always try to make me feel bad when I messed up. People have a misunderstanding of being saved. Just because you are saved it does not exempt you from being attacked by the enemy. As a matter of fact, when we accept Jesus as our Lord and Savior, he gives us a comforter on the inside of us to help fight against every plan of the enemy. Being saved comes from your confession of the mouth and believing in the heart. Early in my walk with Christ, being inexperienced, I fell short of his glory many times. I doubted my salvation and held myself hostage from my mistakes. Watching porn, lying, and letting my anger turn into rage caused me to be stuck in the middle of my transition that brought doubt to my salvation.

Doubt brings use into a spiritual sickness that stops improvement. The devil knows if he can sow a seed of doubt into the human mind, he has a 50% chance of getting us to back-slide. Doubt is a tool of the enemy and is used best when our mind is tossed between that which is real and that which is not.

Romans10:9-10 (KJV) says, if you confess with your mouth The Lord JESUS and believe in your heart that God raised him from the dead, you will be saved.

For with the heart one believes unto righteousness, and with the mouth confession Is made unto Salvation. You must to know in your heart that you are saved. Salvation is not based off what we do.

One thing that I have learned, people will always remind you of who you use to be. The reason for that is to trap you into your today, because tomorrow holds your breakthrough. In this walk with God, you do not have to question yourself if you are saved, the cross defeated it all for God's Glory.

I never thought that someone like me would have a heart to cry out for the wrong that I've done in my life.

The things we go through in life can cause our heart to become closed or opened. The Lord's ways are certainly not like our ways. If you told me 16 years ago that I would be attending church on a regular, I would have told you that you are out of your mind. For God's thoughts are not our thoughts. He has shifted my entire life. One day after a service my spiritual mom told me that God told her to ordain me as a deacon of the church. She said son you are already walking in the shoes of a deacon, go home and research it. Of course, all of this was new to me. So, I went home and stared searching the scriptures on the office of a deacon. The life that I was living matched the word of God. During the service of the ordination tears could not stop flowing from my eyes. I could n`t believe that God could use a person like me.

When God blow on you and clean you up from your yesterday, to move your past. His wind will introduce you to your today. God changed the reality of my future. Even the people that knows you in your process, will be amazed at how God can reintroduce you to the same people that knew you before you got saved. When my wife blew in my mouth before I got saved, I did not understand it, but as I got closer to God, it was a must that it took place in my life. There were some things that God had to breath in me again so that restoration could take place in my life. God used my wife to release himself in me.

NOW, I CAN USE YOU

As time went on. People that knew me before I got saved, begin to hear that I was saved and were preaching the word of God. Many could not wrap their minds around that GOD could use a person as myself, who has done so much wrong. It is true, God uses those who man rejects to bring glory to his name. For man look at the outward appearance, but the Lord looks on the heart. A lot of the guys I left behind began to reach out to me, asking how did I make the change? The first thing that I do is give the glory back to God. I let them know that I'm just an instrument that God is using to release sweet melodies to reach out to his people.

My transition was like a movie. The Lord is using me to win over drug dealers, gang bangers, and a lot of guys that was living the street life. The word of God tells us that they overcame by the blood of the lamb and by the word of their testimony. Revelation 12 :11(KJV). My testimony has given guys hope when they could not see a way out of the reality of what they were living in. God uses testimonies to reassure his people that he has not forgotten about them. One of the biggest robberies the enemy has committed against many people that have overcame by the blood of the lamb and the word of their testimony is by silence. When we become silent about what God has done in our life it discredits God's works. Your testimony is God's assignment for the profile of the kingdom of God.

    I think many people believe that once you get save, you are supposed to hide in the perfection of religion so that no one would know who you used to be or what you used to do. But can I tell you, that we all are an "Ex" Something. I'm a big believer that God allows what you went through to be a blueprint for someone else's life situations. It teaches and shows them that they are not the only ones going through what they are facing. What God delivered you from, he will call you to, so that he can get the glory out of what others have pronounced death to.

    Guys that were once on the opposite ends of the pistol with me, now I find myself praying for them. Giving them words of encouragement, to even calling them on the phone, especially, when I hear that death has struck their family. Many did not want to believe that I changed. They were still stuck in my past. My now was passing them by, and my future has brought me so far that their mind could not see past what I use to be. God was using my testimony. Your testimony will give people hope all around the world. They are just waiting on you to speak about the goodness of the Lord. When we went into the prison to minister. The Lord lead me to share my testimony. Guys that was thinking about giving up, left encourage to KEEP PRESSING. When God place his approval on you, no one can overturn it.

    As a teen I serve the devil with all my strength. As a MAN OF GOD I promise to give the Lord my best and first strength. I continue to serve in my local assembly as my spiritual mother and father help to mature and teach me the ways of the Lord. I got the opportunity to see them in and outside of the church living a life according to the bible. Their lifestyle even helped me to become a better husband to my wife. God began to tell me that he could use me in different methods while still preaching the same message to bring his men to him. A few years back my spiritual mom placed me over our men's ministry. I could see it pulling me out of my comfort zone. There's one thing she said to me that stuck with me and that is, "your ministry will birth out of this." Today, I'm walking in the manifestation of what my spiritual mom spoke over my life. Which carried influence over many men. When I was playing football to hustling in the streets, I had a lot of influence on many young guys. Now as a pastor, the same influence has carried over with even greater responsibility. As a young man, I led with my head which ended with consequences that were no good. Now, I have learned to do it with a heart that exemplifies putting others before myself. It is such a blessing to have God to use you for his glory.

    During our prison ministry at church God used me in the prison to share my life story with the guys that was there. The power of God was very strong in the prison. It saved one of the guys from killing himself, B/C he chose to obey the voice of the Lord as I spoke. While I was ministering The Lord told me that someone was going to commit suicide. The Lord spoke and said "don't do it, the enemy want to kill you in the wilderness before you can truly know who you are." After I was through ministering, a guy came up to me and said it was me who was going to take my life. I told him what The Lord said, and it saved that man from hell that day. Men that threw in the towel, began to say if God did it for you, he can do it for me as I shared my testimony. When we first came into the building, they looked at my outward appearance. They saw a young man with a clean cut from church. You would look at me and assume I grew up in the church. But as I spoke, they knew it was only God that could reach them where they were. That day taught me a valuable lesson. God will use anyone when you make yourself open to his disposal. The men that was in the prison begin to tell us to pray for them. As we looked at the clock our time was up, but the warden gave us extra time to ministry. He seen the power of God move himself. Before we came to that prison, it was known as a place of violence. By the grace of God, we demonstrated what his kingdom was all about. Many got saved and our meeting with them grew significant. My heart beats are for the people that are incarcerated. Thinking about some of the things that I did as a kid could have easily landed me there. That day open my eyes, it was two young guys that looked no more than 15 years old. They ran up to us and said please pray for us, we are tired of this. As we traveled back home from the prison. I could only wonder, what the two young men meant by being tired of this. Both had tears in their eyes. I begin to picture myself as them, because I could have been them.

GOD USES WIVES TO SAVE MAN FROM THEMSELVES

My wife saw me come from the streets to now in the pulpit preaching and living for CHRIST. She's my greatest supporter, encourager, counselor, and friend. God really does use wives to save husbands from their own self destruction. Before I met my wife, I knew that the life that I was living was headed to a dead end. The hurt that I experience from losing my mom, from not being able to play football, and the absence of my father have made me a ticking time bomb. These events caused me to have a I don't care attitude.

A father teaches his son who he will become, by what he sees his father do. When God brought my wife into my life, she gave me a breath of fresh air. The events of my Life were very congested. Meeting my wife was exactly what I needed after the passing of my mother. She could call my name like no one else could and have my undivided attention. My wife reminded me so much of my mom who had a heart for others. She would give you her last, and always willing to help others out. Coming from the lifestyle I lived in the streets made my heart very callous. Disappointments had my heart covered with no feelings. That`s why it was important for my wife to blow into my mouth. As I explained earlier, it was a sign of God bringing restoration to my life.

Life events made my heart so fat, the only thing that could untwist it was God`s divine touch. Growing up my wife and I use to be neighbors. I did n`t think as a young boy that one day we would be married. She really helped me to re-value my life. I was so deep in the streets to the point that I did not care if I lived or died. It was God's will for me to meet my wife and make that transition from a boy into a man. The WORD of God states "As a child I spoke as a child, I understood as a child, as a child I thought as a child, but when I became a man, I put away childish things."

Over the years, it still surprises me how much that we have accomplish as husband and wife. People look at our relationship and marriage and desire what we have. What they don`t see is the work that was put in our marriage privately. Marriage is not just a public act. Over the years I have learned the ones that try to show the most affection in the sight of others have the least private affection when it counts the most (home). God had a different plan for me. I could not see it from beyond the streets, the gang life, and the hurt. God used my wife to save me from prison, early death, and from people who just wanted to use my influence in the wrong way.

Genesis 2 :18 (KJV)… And the LORD said, it is not good that man should be alone, I will make him a help meet for him.

My wife has helped me develop so much as a man that I will forever be in debt to her. I left my home city as a boy and return as a Man of God. Time manifested in seasons that matured me in the areas of my life where I was immature. I learned that time will develop you for purpose, but it will never wait on you.

The Lord joined my wife and I together, teaching us both on how time and responsibility goes hand in hand. We got married at a young age. I remember people telling me, Shawn you are too young for marriage. But can I tell you that today I give counseling to the same people that were against me getting married so young.

My wife was a gift from God to bring balance to my life. In the place where I just knew the street life. She helped to open my eyes to see that it's an entire world out there. If all that you see is one way of living you will develop a close mind. I respect men that can say they became a better person after marrying their wife. Majority of our men have never had a pattern to follow when it comes to becoming a husband. For wives, as young girls, they are in training from the very first time they receive their first doll. They learn the provision of what is necessary for the health, welfare, and maintenance of the family. For husbands, as boys we are given a ball and learn to compete instead of taking care of responsibilities. We go through life competing with other men. We compare ourselves by what we can buy or have. A lot of my friends were the first man in their family to become a husband. Many have shared with me that they are learning to be a husband as they grow with their family.

Some found strength within the counsel of other men, while others look to guys that have never been married. Wives, when you encourage your husband, it speaks to the boy on the inside of him. This gives him superman powers. Besides a man's mother, his wife is the person that can shape him into the person that she wants him to be. If she wants a king, speak to the king within him. If she wants a lazy man don't encourage him and talk down to his every mistake. Husbands your wife was designed by God to make you a better man. King Solomon says, "Houses and riches are an inheritance from fathers, but a prudent wife is from the Lord" (Proverbs 19:1).

God took the two of us and melted us together as one flesh. The bond of marriage is so strong that God intended for it to be broken only by death. Your marriage is what you make it. My wife always encourages me to do and be better. This method has saved countless of men from prison, early death, and have built them to last where others thought they would die.

NOW I CAN TRUST YOU TO GO GET MY PEOPLE

Life was great, I was dedicated to serving in the house of the Lord with my all. I was growing deeper in the Word of God and wanted to save every person that had a similar background as mine. A few years later the Lord spoke to my spiritual mom again about ordaining me as a pastor. She said son you are already doing the work of a pastor. She said, why do you think your heart for the people of God is the way that it is. Seeking a title was not what I was looking for, I just wanted more of God. In the mist of it, God turned my entire life around. I could not believe that all this was happening.

The Lord really put a fire in my belly to go get his people. One day He spoke to me again and said son, I want you to start a prayer group called "LET THE SONS OF GOD ARISE, 100 MEN

IN PRAYER." I took it back to my spiritual mom and she said run with it. Our men's ministry began to engage with other ministries, and we witnessed the fire of God break out in prayer in our region. Men activated in prayer and loved doing it. Then, the Lord told us to take it to the streets. We witnessed the glory of God like we have never seen before. That year over 100 men Gave their lives to Christ. Anytime that we step into a new arena in our lives we've got to allow God to show us and remain teachable. God begin to tell me, now I can trust you to win others because I have restored you from your brokenness. It's amazing how the Lord can take your brokenness, to make someone else whole. Purpose is in your brokenness. Don't throw the pieces away. I heard of GOD as a kid, but I did not have a personal relationship or know him. Through my humbleness, he taught me who He was. From Hustler to Husband, my life has really taken a turn. Even some of the people that knew me before I got saved still can't believe it. I always tell people don' t die in your process, it's just temporary. God sees you as the finished product. So many times, we think that the mistakes that we made in life dictate who we become. Our mistakes work for our future. You will see it again, maturity will have introduced it to time, which will turn your mistake into a launching pad to elevate you for something greater. In order to be great, you got to go through the process and sacrifice of dying to self. The very thing that God kept me from (prison). He allowed me to go there and encourage his sons who have taken and made bad decision in life.

When I was gang banging and hustling people used to tell my Aunt, by the time I turn 20 years old. I would be in one of two places, Dead or in Jail. I beat the odds, because God had something greater for me. Through social media, in person, or whenever I go visit my hometown. I'm able to reach the same people that I used to be at war with. Many times, I prayed for them, encouraged, and we embrace each other with genuine love. All of this was from God trusting me to go get his people. It wasn't because I qualified for the job, but for him to use my imperfection to perfect another person life for his glory. Many of them who have encountered the young version of me, are now witnessing the power of God moving in my life. I have the opportunity and privileged now to mentor some of the same men that I used to run the streets with into being husbands.

HUSTLER TO HUSBAND

A hustler can be anyone of a particular profession who has a mind set to get a job done at any cost. The word Hustler has many definitions. The one that I prefer to use is, an aggressively hard worker, who knows how to get around problems. A hustler can be your doctor, lawyer, or all the way down to your neighborhood candy lady. For me being transformed from a hustler to husband has taught me a lot about myself. I grew up in a household where I saw relationship work, but not marriage. I truly thank the Lord for giving me a wife that has helped groom me to be the husband that I am today. I remember at the age of 24 years old. Standing at the altar with my hands sweating, throat dry, and nervous. I was about to enter into one of the best moments of my life, but fearful!!! "Did I really have what it takes to be a husband?" I can truly say if our marriage had not been built on the foundation of the Lord, we would have not made it over the last 15 years of marriage and 19 years all together. All of this was for the preparation of where we stand today.

Now teaching marriage ministry at our local church and it feels so good because we can be transparent with the other married couples about the good and bad in marriage. B/C people go into it after the honeymoon stage which they plan on living until life happens. Some couples get stronger while others find themselves divorce. Once we went to a marriage seminar. Some of the people that was there have been married for 30 years, 20 years, 10 years, 5 years, 1 year and even down to 3 months was experiencing some of the same issues in marriage. For my wife and I, it exposed us to another level of Love. A lot of people see us in our now and may want what we have, but the true is, God ordain us for each other.

My wife was a woman who saw me beyond where I was. She got a chance to see how the Lord change me from a hustler to a husband. Now she gets to enjoy the fruit of what she has prayed for. One of the biggest problems that many have in marriages are comparing their spouse to other married couples. (2 Corinthians 10:12) states that it's not wise to compare ourselves. We should measure our marriage to itself, it will show us where we need improvement at. I got to admit when I first got married, I walked into it fearful. This was something that I have never witnessed firsthand. I didn't have the first clue on how to be a husband. The Lord began to teach me the what's, when's, how's, and responsibilities of being a husband.

The word husband comes from the two words house and band, meaning to keep together. This applies to a strip of metal or rope used to bind houses together. I came from a background where women kept the house banded together and now to be in a leadership role of keeping a house banded together was new to me. But as time went on, I notice that my "what" began to change, God taught me the "when" in the marriage, the "how" to handle things in and out of the marriage, and responsibilities.

When the first husband was created Adam, God gave him a clear self-image. He knew that he was the image of God and who he was. He was not intimidated by others. The identity of man goes back to the image of God's D.N.A. Transforming from a hustler in the streets into a husband meant God had to rebuild my foundation. Many husbands miss God in their marriage because they don`t know the purpose of allowing God to build them from his foundation and will. So, a great deal of men enter marriage misusing the very thing that God has given as a gift. I remember first going into marriage. I heard a MAN OF GOD say, when he first got married, he believed that God made a mistake. His wife could n`t cook. He always put her down with his words. Even as a MAN OF GOD, he understood that death and life are in the power of the tongue and they that love it shall eat the fruit thereof (Proverbs 18:21.) The more he talked bad about his wife cooking, the worse it got. He was eating the fruit of what he created with his words. One day he said God convicted him of how he was treating and talking to his wife. Immediately he apologized to her and change the words that he was speaking to his wife. He said as time went on the food started to taste better by the day. This happens a lot in marriages Because many men never ask the Lord for direction in their marriage.

Psalm 127:1 (Msg. Bible) reads, If God does not build the house, the builder's only build shacks.

Many people go into marriage with a shack mind set. Not knowing it's just temporary because God is not in it. When we allow God to be the foundation of our marriage, what we did not learn, he will teach us. The second thing, as a husband God wants us to spend time in his presence. In Genesis 2:8 the Bible tells us that God planted a garden eastward in Eden which means presence, and there he put the man whom he formed. God placed Adam in his sanctuary (his presence) so that Adam would know his voice. Adam was so connected to God that the voice of God used to walk before him. Even In my walk with the Lord through worship, prayer, and in my quiet time I could hear the voice of God walking with me as I spent time in his presence.

When I feel low, I turn on some instrumental worship music and it refreshes me, because times of refreshing comes from being in the presence of the Lord. As a husband the more time we spend in the presence of God, the hard places in our heart that we don't let anyone in, God will begin to massage it. Many men have never heard the voice of a physical father or spent time in his presence. Which makes it hard for them to spend time in God's presence. They begin to compare God with their own biological fathers who was absent in their life. Once a husband understands the importance of the presence of God, he would seek him the more.

The third thing that God commanded the first husband to do was to work. He gave Adam the garden to dress it which means to work. 2 Thessalonians 3:10 states that… If any man would not work, neither should he eat. We live in a time where many men are not working, and they've allowed their wives to go out to bring the beacon home, while they stay at home and play video games. When God birthed Eve out of the side of Adam, as he presented her to Adam who was already working. From the lack of influence from the older husbands many younger husbands have taken on this new trend of not working. They tend to just let their wives go out to work. This has shifted the entire order of the house that God has ordained.

    Even before I got saved, I had a passion to work. My wife told me that's one of the reasons why she married me. She knew that I would work for our family. A lot of young husbands were raised by their mother and going into marriage they are not looking for a wife, but a mother. Yes, they love them, but they have the concept of their wife doing the things that their mother used to do for them as a boy. When I was hustling the majority of my friends I hung with did not have a male role model in their life to teach them the role of a man working. The men who received respect were the older drug dealers. They did not clock into a 9-5 job but hustled to get what they got. As I look back at it, they loved to put you on which means (give you drugs to sell to get started) but they will not teach you how to fill out a job application.

    Now that I'm grown, I see that many never worked because they had no one to push them. So, as they became grown men, they just followed the trend. Many guys think that this is the life until they go to prison and end up working for cents per hour. When I was blind, I did not see it like this. You will work in the free world or you will work in prison. I have witnessed some of the biggest drug dealers go from having a lot of money from hustling, to getting locked up. When released from prison working jobs that they would have never work before going to prison. To my brothers, work. God set this order in the home that you would be a provider for your family.

"Remember a man does not work, a man does not eat."

The fourth thing that God told Adam to do as a husband was to cultivate the garden. Which means to improve his surroundings (family). As husbands, God gave us a leadership role when he told Adam to name the animals and whatever name that he gave it that is its name. God called us into marriage so that we would not take anything away from our wives, but to bring increase them. Most men don't understand that their wives are the reflection of them. If they take from her, they are subtracting from themselves.

A wise man builds his house upon the rocks so when the storms of life come, he would be safe. He understands the stronger his surroundings are, he's able to overcome the toughest challenges in the different seasons of life. A foolish man will build his house on sand, not improving in the areas where he needs work, but wait until the storm of life hit his home. The lack of improvement will cause it to be carried away with the rain and wind of the storms of life.

The fifth thing that God told Adam to do was guard the garden. As husbands our duty is to protect our families at any cost. This is so critical that God said it in (Ephesians 5:25) Husbands, love your wives, just as Christ also loved the church, and gave himself for it. We should be willing to die for our wives or family. A true man will protect, he will not violate his wife, he will not hurt her with his words, physically, or mentally. His job is to protect everything that's under his care. Husbands remember God gave you that family to oversee. As the protector, you are responsible for every individual. This is something that I take to heart when it comes to my wife. I do not disrespect her and there's no way that I would allow anyone else to.

The sixth thing that God gave Adam the husband was his word. Men are called to be the 5 P's in marriage

1. Provider
2. Protector
3. Prophet
4. Promoter
5. Priest.

How can we be all of these if we never spend time in his presence? We as men are to come before the Lord and release his word back to our family. It's our job to teach his word to our family. One thing that I have noticed is the enemy has stolen the identity of the man in the family and replaced it with things. We live in a time where men have adopted sports, their job, and their man caves as their god. We have replaced the word of God with activities and hobbies. In society, when you try to talk with guys about The Lord, one of the most popular things that they say is "Man I`m not ready yet"." A lot of men do not understand that his entire family is wrapped up in his not ready yet mindset. Coming from an Ex. Hustler, if you are not talking to your kids about the Lord, I promise you, someone else is talking to them about other things that will cost you as a family.

When I left home at the age 16 years old, I did not understand what I was doing. Later, I realize that I did not only leave home. I left from under the covering of my stepdad. As a man we are umbrellas of our family. Meaning, one of our responsibilities to our families is to be the cover them from any harm or danger. This duty of covering our family keeps them from getting wet from the storms of life. In the natural, when it rains and if you don`t have an umbrella you get wet. With an umbrella, our chances are slim to getting wet. God set this order when Eve ate of the forbidden fruit. He placed the man over the woman, and God is over the man. This gives accountability to the family. I had to learn this the hard way when I left home at 16 years old. The storms of life had me drowning and I was n`t even aware of it. My storm was the streets and everything that came with it.

STREETS TO THE PULPIT (SAVED BY GRACE)

Everything that I went through God has graced me for. 2 Corinthians 12:9 (KJV) states… And he said unto me, my grace is sufficient for thee, for my strength is made perfect in weakness. Most gladly therefore will I rather glory in my infirmities, that the power of CHRIST may rest upon me. All along God has his hand on me so that he can use me for his glory. Of all that I've been through and of all the things I've done. I survived by His Grace. "<u>G</u>od's <u>R</u>iches <u>a</u>t <u>C</u>hrists' <u>E</u>xpense." When the streets tried to kill me on numerous occasions, I used to think I got away by luck. But there's no such thing as luck in God. I was wrapped in His unmerited favor.

The supper natural strength of God helped me where my decisions caused restriction in my life. Before I got saved, I use to think that church was just a gimmick, until I met my spiritual mom and church family. I have so much respect for my spiritual mom.

She ordained me and never looked for the approval of men. Eight years later, she ordained me as pastor. She is the type of person who seeks God and obeys his voice. My spiritual mom did not let what I had been through hold me hostage to my destiny.

One of the things that shifted me from my old church before I came to where I'm at today is the comments about my dreadlocks. They were more concerned with what others would think of my appearance than getting to know my heart. This left a bad taste in my mouth about church. All that changed when I meet my spiritual parents. Their love and from the church were authentic.

They showed love, taught truth, and not religion. I witness the love, truth, and power of Christ which he gave us a leader after his own heart. My spiritual mom has taught me so much about The Lord. Never once did I think that God could take a kid from the streets who did not know him and place them behind the pulpit. The streets will lie to you with a false pretense that everything you see is real. As a man of God, I have learned that Jesus is the complete revelation of grace from God the father.

Ephesians 2: 8-9 says...
8. For by grace are ye saved through faith, and that not of yourselves, it Is the gift of God. 9. Not of works, lest any man should boast.

God gave us grace so that it will keep us moving as father's, leaders, businessman, and priest in our homes. Grace is the only solution for the evilness of mankind. The more I grew in the Lord he taught me that grace disqualifies excuses. From the streets when things went wrong, we always look for an excuse to blame others. Grace was my defense even when I could not see that it was protecting me. Every day I thank God for keeping me even when I did not deserve to be kept.

Most guys from the streets believe in the Lord, but very few believe in real Men of GOD. The reason why, is that a lot man become saved and show perfection and don't share their imperfection. This attitude scares men from the house of God B/C they know that they don't have it all together. When the Lord allowed me to go back to my hometown preaching peace and unity. When the community were faced with violence which lead to a lot of killing. It changed a lot of the guys heart and mentality. The last time many seen me I was engaging in the violence, but now against it. Many knew me from the streets and to now seeing me behind the pulpit gives them hope. I am always asked, how I did it and my reply is "ALL GLORY GOES TO GOD." I won't dare take the credit for what God has done. Remember early in the book, my plan for moving was to find a drug connection, but in the mist, I found the ultimate connection JESUS CHRIST. The Lord taught me that he will take an average guy from the streets, and put his anointing on him, so that he can get the glory.

1 Corinthians 1: 25 -28 (KJV) 25. Because the foolish of God Is wiser than men, and the weakness of God Is stronger than men. 26. For ye see your calling, brethren, how that not many wise men after the flesh, not many mighty, not many noble, are called. 27. But God hath chosen the foolish things of the world to confound the wise, and God hath chosen the weak things of the world to confound the things which are mighty. 28. And base things of the world and things which are despised hath God chosen yea and things which are not, to bring to naught things that are.

BONUS : WIFE OF A HUSTLER

Hello everyone! I guess it is time for me to tell my side of the story, so here it goes; I want to start out by saying I have literally known my Husband all my life, why I say that, well I am glad you ask. My Husband and I grew up together, we were neighbors since I were 7 years old. We hung out in same area together, played together, he hung with my brother, my Family knew his family, my mom and his aunt used to hang out together as well. I never thought that, He would one day be my husband, honestly; the thought never crossed my mind. We grew up together we were neighbors never dated or anything just kids playing or seeing each other in the neighborhood having a good time. But God had another plan for us. Who have thought that one day he would be my husband?

Let's fast forward till the moment that we actually started talking, so what happen...I was at a club with my cousins and I instantly from afar seen him and I knew it was him, I walked up to him just to speak, because I knew him and consider him as a friend from the neighborhood. I said Hi, how you doing? what's going on? Have not seen you in a long time and I asked him if he remembered my cousin, that type of nature just simple chit chat. The following week I seen him again at the basketball game. I said we keep bumping into each other, this the most I've seen you in years and that was it! My cousin and I walked away; so, when I walked away in that moment, not knowing it then but he told me later that when I walked away from speaking to him in his mind he was saying oh yeah ,I got to have her. I wasn't even trying to date anyone, but He found me. I was simply speaking to a childhood friend.

That, following Monday I got a phone call from Him, I was like who is this, he told me who he were, and I asked how did you get my number? I never gave him my phone number; I may have been a little offensive, but I was really trying to figure out how He get my number, no one really had my number it was new. Once he told me my friend from school, she gave it to him. He was like oh! you didn't want me to call you. I laugh and said it's cool, at that moment I knew he liked me. We've been talking ever since. When we met, I remember he was a hustle all about the street life (drugs, gang, etc.) I knew the street because I grew up in them, we hung out, drunk alcohol and smoked weed on the regular, what else is there to do in our small town and of course play cards, but I wasn't no hustle I rather work. I saw so many get caught up in the hustle life and I learn quickly that I love my freedom and my life, plus I knew God had more for me to do, so after dating him for a couple of years, I was done with the lifestyle looking over your shoulder, not being able to trust people, dealing with stiches, fake friends and untrustworthy family having to sleep half-awake in fear of your door would be kicked in. The whole system that comes with the hustle of any streets. God was frustrating me so much that I broke down one day talking to my friend crying and all I said I got to leave here, God is pushing me to go. I feel so stuck this is not it! (IT GOT TO BE MORE THAN THIS!) I came home told him I am moving God said for me to go, I always believe in God the father of Jesus Christ but never had a real relationship with him, I just knew he was real and always with me in every step of my life, my grandmother raised me to Trust God and would take me to church with her but I never had my own experience with God, but that day I heard him clearly saying to me: If you stay you will die. Weather he meant physically or spiritually I did n ' t know I just knew what he said and at that time I thought he meant physically, and I wanted to live. I told my Husband who was my boyfriend at the time, and he was like, why we good, you can go I'm straight, are you sure? Listen, I never been more certain in my life. I pack my bags called my God brother and off to the bus station, I went I only had $50.00 and a bag of clothes. I thought it only cost $49.00 that's what the TV said anywhere on the bus for 49.00 but I didn't know it had to be purchase in advance, so the cost was $89.00 when I arrived at the bus station. I was so determined not to go, I told my brother to go ahead I am not leaving if I have to ask everyone who walk by for $5.00 I was getting on that bus, my brother said sis here you go. He gave me $50.00 dollars God is always on time. Fast forward within 30 days of being in a new state, I had a job, my own apartment and two cars to drive. I came back with a U-Haul to pick up my stuff when I got home, he wasn't there so both my brothers started loading the truck while we were packing, he came and asked what was I doing? I said I am leaving I am not telling you to go nor am I telling you to stay, the choice is yours this is your life here, not mines. We talked and he said he had a couple of things to handle and once I got settled he would come. We all loaded the truck and the very next morning I was gone. I told him if you do come, this life must be left behind, I am not living like this anymore! He agreed. Later, I found out, he had no intention of leaving that hustle lifestyle behind, in fact he was only coming to find a connect but instead he found God. It was not easy, I have to tell you my whole story another time, it took almost 6 years later until God answer my prayers. I don't have enough time to tell you what it took to see him to become the Husband he is today. My lifestyle was what influence him to change, He seen me serve God for real and even when I messed up, he seen me never give up, I kept going even through the many mistakes I made. I will never say to anyone I got this, or I made it because I know the spirit is willing, but the flesh is so weak. What I will say is our love for each other has stood the test of it all the good, bad, truth, and lies. Coming from nothing to having something together keeps us humble and grateful that He is able…A wife you instantly want your husband to change and you think nagging and arguing is the key to make them listen, true story I was praying because now we go to church, and all I want is his presence, not sure if you ever got save but that first time is a high that is unexplainable all you want is more of God so we would go to church. I could tell he only went because I wanted him to go so I am praying God get him, change him lord, God you got to help me and God said to me YOU need to change first, He asked me what drew me to him, I said the love my pastor wife showed me and He said that's the same thing that will draw him to me. I didn't realize that I was at that moment the only Jesus he knew threw me and my actions will either draw him to God or away from God. God said just pray and let your life speak. I stop trying to force the word on him and stop looking for all his mistakes and begin to focus on the good and God began to show me the husband trapped inside the Hustle. I began to treat him as my husband and the man whom God chose for me. I couldn't have asked for a better husband; he is perfect for Me! I know it takes the right kind of man for me and he is it! My husband whom I watched changed before my very eyes, I always knew that God hand was on him and Greatness was in him. I am honored to be your helpmate to help push you to be the Man of God and complete the purpose of God in your life. My Husband that you are Today, this is that which He was spoken of. When everyone else counted you out I was including you in my life and we have just began....friends forever and lovers always. Power of two!

Made in the USA
Columbia, SC
28 July 2019